SEVEN SECRETS FOR
SUCCESS
IN THE WORKPLACE

H. David Schuringa

CBI Publishing Center
P.O. Box 900
Grand Rapids, MI 49509-0900
www.cbi.fm

What bosses wish
their employees knew.

TABLE OF CONTENTS

The Work Ethic Is Not about Your Paycheck

The Work Ethic Shapes Your Character

The Work Ethic Defines Your Purpose

The Work Ethic Directs You on the Road
   to Success

The Work Ethic Identifies Your Real Boss

Why Arrive Early?

Cultural Perceptions

Hey, What about My Pay?

A Better Way

No Complaining Allowed

But Most People Hate Their Jobs, Right?

Positive People Are Happier and Healthier

Be Positive about Criticism!

Become the Top Promoter

Let Go of Your Balloon

Hints in the Handbook

All employers are looking for the same basic things in an employee.

> *Well-meaning individuals are sabotaging themselves at work without even knowing it.*

INTRODUCTION

Thousands of people are sabotaging themselves at work without even knowing it. Take the young attendant on a smoke break who I overheard as I was coming out of the gas station. He was chatting with his friend.

"This new job is great," he said.

"Good," I thought, "a young man with the work ethic!" But then, my hopes were dashed to pieces.

"We work 12-hour shifts. Only have to suffer for three days, and then the rest of the week is ours!"

Suffer? Is that how he thinks of work? I guess so. And I don't think he is alone in thinking of work as "suffering."

"Work as suffering." Quite a concept. And too bad! If only he could see his work as reflecting the image of God in him.

After all, God works.

He worked before time began, making his plan (Ephesians 1:5, 11). Then, in history he worked to bring this plan to life. He worked six days in creating the world (Genesis 1:31) and continues to work today, in his divine providence governing the world and working out all things for the good of those who love him (Ephesians 1:11; Romans 8:28).

God the Son worked alongside him in creation (John 1:3) and then came into the world, sent by his father to do the work of salvation (John 5:36). He continues to work at his father's right hand, ruling over all things (Ephesians 1:22) and interceding on our behalf (Hebrews 7:25). One day, he will come again to do the work of renewing the world (Revelation 21:5).

God the Holy Spirit is also busy indeed, accomplishing the work of salvation in us (Galatians 4:6; 1 John 3:24).

And so we find that God works, and we have been created in his image to work as well (Genesis 1:27). When we understand this, a transformation takes place. Work as a cause for suffering becomes work as a thrilling and fulfilling adventure as we help create a world that is a better place in which to live.

But now we are getting ahead of ourselves.

The young man to whom I referred is heading for a dreary life. Without the work ethic, he will be trapped in the self-fulfilling prophesy of work understood as suffering. And in days of high unemployment, recessionary blues and stiff competition, he will undoubtedly suffer. He desperately needs this book!

However, even if you have already experienced some degree of success in the workplace, this book will serve as a useful refresher course, helping to strengthen any weak areas you might have. Since many of the topics in the book lend themselves to small group discussion, you may even want to use it with a study group at work, church or school.

But this book is not only for employees who want to be more successful. It is also useful for employers in corporations, businesses and non-profits.

It is important for you to know that your boss really does want you to succeed at your work. You see, if you succeed, your boss succeeds. It's a win-win situation! In this book, you too can discover the seven secrets that successful employers and employees use to thrive in the workplace. If these strategies can be helpful to you or someone you know, then I'm thankful for the opportunity to share them with you.

Over the years, I've learned a few things about the importance of a strong work ethic. I first learned many of these secrets from my parents, who taught me the value of hard work. Later, as an employee I learned by trial and error in various jobs and from discussions with employers.

In addition to being an employee myself, I've been an employer for many years. In the business and non-profit worlds, I've seen firsthand the difference between a successful employee who knows the secrets for success in the workplace and one who struggles and fails. I know what bosses wish their employees knew, because I know what I look for in an outstanding employee. I've consulted with other employers, and I've found that, while job duties may vary, all employers are looking for the same basic qualities in an employee. That's why they want you to know the secrets.

Finally, the strategies I lay out in this book come from more than my experience as an employee and an employer. Both formally and informally, I'm a student of religion, which has a lot to say on the subject of work. While I'll be approaching the topic of work primarily from a Christian perspective, it will be interesting to note that many religions have similar things to say when it comes to the ethics of work. Because people are spiritual beings, I believe it is important to take into account the spiritual dimension of work.

Think of the work ethic as a recipe and each secret in this book as an ingredient in the recipe. While many people in the workplace are following a recipe for disaster, it doesn't have to be that way. If you carefully study each ingredient I share here and follow this recipe, I guarantee you will be better equipped to succeed in the workplace.

Your work does not have to be a form of suffering like the young gas station attendant's. It can be a great joy and a source of fulfillment for you as you work in reflection of the image of God within you.

SECRET 1

Change the Way You Think about Your Work!

SECRET 1:

Change the Way You Think about Your Work!

One of the most important factors that will contribute to your success in life is getting and keeping a job. In addition to causing obvious financial difficulties, failing in the workplace can lead to other serious problems. In fact, roughly 80% of currently imprisoned people were either unemployed or underemployed (earning annual wages below the poverty level) when they committed their crimes. As you can see, being unemployed can get you into trouble.

I believe that one of the greatest crises of Western culture is a diminishing work ethic. Whether this is due to our growing prosperity or increasingly poor

> *One of the greatest crises of Western culture is a diminishing work ethic.*

training, it's clear that the workforce has grown soft and lazy and has developed an attitude of entitlement. This is killing us in the workplace, dulling our competitive edge in the global market and spiritually destroying our society as we miss out on the joy of work.

The *joy* of work?

This phrase might have caught you off guard, but most people can probably think of work that they actually like to do. For some it may be gardening, for others fixing up the car or cooking. It all depends on your attitude and perspective; we just usually don't call things we like doing "work." The fact is that if we go about it in the right way, our work not only can be enjoyable but also can bring meaning to our lives. That's why the first secret for success in the workplace is to change the way you think about your work. Everyone needs the work ethic.

The Work Ethic Is Not about Your Paycheck
If you ask people on the street why they work, they will likely say, "To pay the bills." The fact is that

receiving a paycheck is a *result* of our work, but should never be the primary *reason* we work.

People working merely for a paycheck tend to drift aimlessly from job to job, from paycheck to paycheck, wondering why they don't get anywhere in life. On the other hand, those who understand the work ethic tend to get ahead in life because they are working for a different reason.

Excellent workers understand the work ethic. Since such employees are hard to find today, employers can spot them a mile away. When someone who "gets it" comes along, that person usually moves up the ladder quickly because employers don't want to lose someone who understands the work ethic. Sure, there are bosses who promote for the wrong reasons, but most dream of a team that has the work ethic.

The idea that work is infinitely more than a paycheck is not a recent invention, but is an idea that goes back deep into world history. According to sociologist Max Weber, the work ethic was rediscovered in Western civilization at the time of the Reformation in the 16th century. Weber especially credits

John Calvin with this discovery. Perhaps you've heard of the Protestant or Calvinist work ethic. As followers of Calvin, the Puritans brought this ethic to America, so some now call it the American work ethic.

This work ethic was "rediscovered" at the time of the Reformation because it can be traced in history back to the Middle East and the early beginnings of the Judeo-Christian heritage. The work ethic in the Hebrew Scriptures began with Moses, who was probably born around 1400 BC.

The work ethic also emerged independently in the Far East. Tradition holds that Confucius was born around 551 BC, and his writings reveal a strong work ethic. Since many other Eastern religions are influenced by Confucianism, it should come as no surprise that the work ethic has also left an imprint in religions such as Buddhism and Hinduism.

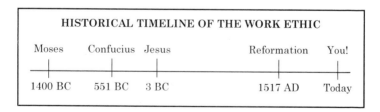

HISTORICAL TIMELINE OF THE WORK ETHIC

Moses	Confucius	Jesus		Reformation	You!
1400 BC	551 BC	3 BC		1517 AD	Today

The fact is that we can find the work ethic in many cultures and religions around the world, and all are in agreement that work should not be about the paycheck. So, even today, some of the greatest

> *The work ethic is a
> divinely revealed moral
> code for the workplace.*

philosophers in world history can positively impact
your thinking about your work!

The Work Ethic Shapes Your Character

Why is it called the work "ethic"? Ethics involves a
moral code by which one lives life. Ethics tells us
about the right and wrong way of doing things,
whether it be how we conduct ourselves in personal
relationships, how we handle our finances or even
our attitude regarding the environment.

The work ethic, then, has to do with a moral code
for your work. In the same way we consider
immoral those who cheat on their spouses, we could
also say that those who do not have the work ethic
are immoral or unethical.

The work ethic is a *divinely revealed* moral code for
the workplace. That is why religious traditions have
so much to say about our work. In fact, in the first
chapters of the Hebrew Scriptures, the work ethic is
introduced.

God himself is presented as a worker in Genesis
2:2-3. After creating the world, God created
humans in his image (Genesis 1:27), and he gave

them charge over everything on earth (Genesis 1:28-29). This is often referred to as the "cultural mandate." The second chapter of Genesis explicitly emphasizes the fact that God created people to work (Genesis 2:15). In other words, God gave us work to do. Subsequent Scriptures tell us *how* God intends us to work.

There is, then, a divinely revealed moral basis for your work, which, to the extent it is embraced, defines your character—what kind of person you are—because God instructed mankind to work at the dawn of human history.

The Work Ethic Defines Your Purpose
The work ethic is considerably more than a moral obligation; it also has to do with finding purpose and meaning in your life.

Did you know you are hard-wired for work? You might say God planted work in your DNA. That means you will never experience happiness and fulfillment unless you fulfill *your* role in the cultural mandate. That's because the moral code for the workplace is a law anchored in the structures of creation itself. Fighting it or resisting it would be like fighting gravity. You'll never win. In fact, if you try to resist the mandate for work, you will be quite miserable.

As Calvin observes, "We know that man was created with this in view, that he might do something."[1] According to the Talmud, "Great is labor, it confers honor on the laborer." You see, you were designed to succeed in your work.

You were designed not only to enjoy your work but also the *fruit* of your labor from the abundance of the creation. Just listen to what Calvin says in his commentary on the cultural mandate:

> God certainly did not intend that man
> should be sparingly sustained; but rather,
> by these words, he promises a generous
> abundance, which leaves nothing lacking
> for a sweet and pleasant life.[2]

Embracing the work ethic means aligning yourself with how you were wired, and, insofar as you do, it will empower you to experience immense satisfaction and meaning in your life. Fighting your purpose to work can only result in debilitating frustration and failure. Individuals and even entire cultures that lack or lose the work ethic will suffer as a result of missing their purpose in life.

The Work Ethic Directs You on the Road to Success

Maybe you are feeling frustrated that the work ethic requires a complete change in your thinking about your work. Maybe you wish you could buck against this system. If so, you're not alone. The fact is that by nature we've all traveled on the road to failure rather than success.

We come by this naturally because this misdirection began with our first parents in the Garden of Eden. Adam and Eve had the perfect boss, perfect working conditions and perfect wages: the riches of abundant life—everything that would lead to success. But they chose to head in a different direction.

They rebelled against God, and as a result, Adam's guilt and propensity for failure on the job was passed on to us all (Romans 5:12). After the fall into sin, God reaffirmed that man's created purpose was to work. Sin, however, would make his work much more difficult, even painful (cf. Genesis 3:17). Though God fired Adam and Eve from their positions in the garden, work remained the plan for man.

But with the bad news came good news. God promised in Genesis 3:15 that the seed of the woman would ultimately prevail over the seed of the serpent (Satan). This happened when Jesus came to finish his father's work (John 4:34; 5:36; 9:4).

Because of Christ's work on your behalf, you have been redeemed to go in the right direction, to do the work you were intended to do. Despite our failure to be the kind of workers we ought, we can truly enjoy our work as God empowers us to do it. You can get back on the road to success as God intended. The work ethic points the way.

The Work Ethic Identifies Your Real Boss

On the road to success, go about your work as if God were your boss. "Whatever you do, work at it with all your heart, as working for the Lord, not for men" (Colossians 3:23). The work ethic is not only *divinely revealed,* it is also *divinely directed*, i.e. directed toward God.

There's a Hindu proverb that says, "Work is worship." The work ethic as defined by Christianity also holds that our work is worship in that it is the fruit of gratitude for what God has done for us in the perfect and finished work of Jesus Christ.

When we speak of God being your boss, it does not mean that you can sometimes ignore the directions of your earthly boss because you have a heavenly boss giving you orders. Quite the contrary! When you work as if God were your boss, then you will seek to be the best employee an earthly boss could ever have. It also gives you confidence and pause to know that your boss in heaven sees the effort you put forth in ways your earthly boss could never imagine.

It should come as no surprise, then, that the work ethic which puts you on the road to success will inspire you to remain diligent your entire life, as you are able, as long as God gives you breath. Calvin notes the following:

> Let each of us remember, that he has been created by God for the purpose of laboring, and of being vigorously employed in his work; and that not only for a limited time, but till death itself...[3]

So much for the idea that we earn the right to be lazy when we have accumulated sufficient wealth. So much for the idea that retirement is just about relaxing! You can't "retire" from being useful when that is the reason God put you on this planet! And, ultimately, this usefulness will bring you the most satisfaction and pleasure—no matter how old you are.

The secret to arriving at the destination of success in the workplace is to have the work ethic, to follow your heavenly boss by diligently doing the work for which you were intended as long as you are on life's journey.

> **Definition:** *The work ethic is that divinely revealed moral code for the workplace which, insofar as you align yourself with it, will empower you to fulfill your purpose in work that will lead to your success.*

Key Ideas from Chapter 1

📁 The first secret for success in the workplace is to change the way you think about your work by understanding the work ethic.

📁 Receiving a paycheck should never be the primary *reason* we work, but rather a *result* of our work.

📁 The work ethic is a moral code for your work.

📁 In the cultural mandate, God instructed mankind to work. Through fulfilling this mandate, you will experience happiness and contentment.

📁 By nature we have all failed in our work and in understanding our work as we ought.

📁 You can get back on the road to success in life. The work ethic points the way.

📁 The work ethic is not only *divinely revealed*, it is also *divinely directed*, i.e. directed toward God.

📁 Work is worship in that it is the fruit of gratitude for what God has done for us.

📁 We do not earn the right to be lazy once we have accumulated sufficient wealth.

SECRET 2

Never Be on Time

SECRET 2:

Never Be on Time

Yes, you read that correctly. To be a success on the job, you should never be on time—always be early. Rick Pitino, a successful basketball coach, puts it even more strongly when he says that coming to work on time is a *bad habit* you need to break![4]

This key to success doesn't even cross the minds of most employees. In fact, the work ethic makes a difference at the very beginning of every day on the job.

As an employer, I find it absolutely incredible that people think they can succeed while not showing up on time to work, let alone without coming early to work. Apparently some people think that as long as they usually arrive on time or not too late, they are fine.

Wrong.

You should never, ever arrive merely on time, and you should definitely never arrive late, unless there are extenuating circumstances beyond your control. And those ought to be extremely rare, or your life is out of control.

Why Arrive Early?
Arriving early has many advantages:

1. Early arrival says you are eager and excited to be at work.

2. Early arrival tells your boss that this job is a *priority* in your life and shows that you are willing to arrange your schedule and manage your life so you can be at your work early and ready to start.

3. Early arrival gives you time to *prepare* for your day's work; essentially, arriving early shows you are a person who is on the ball and getting somewhere in life.

4. Early arrival gives you time to greet your fellow workers and grab a cup of coffee

> *Do you think an athlete would show up to an event without having stretched or warmed up?*

before work begins, instead of getting settled and chitchatting on company time.

5. Early arrival is handy because it ensures you won't be late even if something (like a flat tire, unexpected traffic backups or inclement weather) goes wrong on the way to work.

6. Early arrival shows you have the work ethic!

Someone who knows the secrets for success on the job can't wait to get up early in the morning and get to work to take on another day! The same attitude goes for those in second and third shifts.

As Coach Pitino asks, do you think an athlete would show up a couple of minutes before the event without having stretched or warmed up? Would a professional golfer arrive at the course at the last minute and just walk up to the tee? Would a singer walk out on stage and start singing without doing her voice exercises?[5] Any champion would arrive plenty early to warm up and get physically and mentally prepared for the game. You ought to do the same if you want to be a winner at work.

As part and parcel of the work ethic, arriving early models virtues such as preparedness, reliability, self-discipline, respect for others, trustworthiness and courtesy. Early arrivers are cut from a special cloth and help cultivate a culture of character in the workplace. Early arrival shows you are going to do your best work, and employers seek to hire and promote people with these virtues.

Cultural Perceptions
Because of cultural backgrounds, the importance of arriving early may not be apparent to some readers. Sociologists recognize that some cultures are "event-oriented" and others are "time-oriented." Depending on your cultural background and the culture in which you work, you may have to adjust your arrival-time habits.

People from cultures that are event-oriented tend to arrive late at events without thinking a thing about it. In these cultures, people may dribble in for an hour or two after the scheduled start time for the event. No one seems to mind, because in these cultures, the event is the most important thing. The assumption is, "When everyone finally arrives, we'll start, and we will continue the event as long as people want to stick around." In event-oriented cultures, the focus is on *the event,* and there seems to be hardly any concept of punctuality.

On the other hand, cultures that are time-oriented
have a very different understanding of timekeeping.
These cultures are oriented to the clock, like to
start things "on time" and expect people to be punc-
tual. In fact, people from these cultures usually
arrive not simply "on time" but even a little early
to an event, whether a church service, a birthday
party or a lunch date. In a time-oriented culture,
people who arrive late will apologize profusely.

Why apologize?

In a time-oriented culture, the start time of an
event is very important. People place a high value
on their time, so arriving late indicates a serious
lack of respect for others. If you agreed to meet at a
certain time and arrived late, you didn't keep your
word, in effect saying, "Your time is not valuable; it
doesn't hurt if you sit here and wait for me. You
have nothing better to do."

When you arrive at the last minute or late to your
job, you are communicating to your boss, "I have no
respect for you or this job." Is that really the mes-
sage you want to send?

Arriving late also shows a lack of humility. In effect you are saying, "I'm more important than you, and I have such important things to do, you can wait for me." The President of the United States may be late and may make people wait. But you are probably not the President of the United States, and you are most likely not more important in the workplace than your boss.

Differences of culture are important to consider. If you come from an event-oriented background but your workplace (your boss) is from a time-oriented culture, there are going to be big problems unless you accommodate to your boss' perception of time.

If you are from an event-oriented culture, your natural inclination may be to say, "What's the big deal, anyway? I'm coming to work; that's all that matters." But, believe me, arriving late is a *huge* deal, and you need to change your habits if you want to succeed! You must learn to show respect for your boss and commitment to your job by adapting to the culture of your workplace. In the United States, for example, it's best to assume that your workplace is a time-oriented culture.

Hey, What about My Pay?
A common, almost predictable objection people have to the discipline of early arrival is this question: "What about my pay? If I don't get paid for early

arrival, I should not have to arrive before starting time. If arriving late is stealing from my employer, isn't arriving early without reimbursement stealing from *me*?"

This kind of thinking will get you nowhere. If you consistently arrive early to work, you will be amply rewarded soon enough (provided you also follow the other secrets I'm sharing with you!).

Let me let you in on a secret: to worry about whether you are going to get paid for early arrival is to be penny wise and dollar foolish. Think of your early arrival as an *investment* in your future success. In the big picture, early arrival will pay handsome dividends.

How early does your boss want you to arrive? Coach Pitino suggests at least 30 minutes. I usually arrive at work 45 to 60 minutes before the office opens, often earlier, and I recommend that the average employee arrive at work at least a few minutes early. Be sure never to arrive late or show up at the last minute.

If your organization does not allow you to "punch in" early, don't officially check in until starting time. But get there early anyway. Your boss will notice your effort. If you *really* want to make a positive impression, make sure you are *never* the last to arrive or the first to leave at the end of the shift.

A Better Way

Arriving early may well require a change in life-style for you. For example, a good share of the workforce stays up late watching television, plops exhausted into bed, gets up the next morning after slamming the snooze button ten times, skips break-fast, breaks the speed limit and rushes into the workplace, huffing, puffing and sweating, to punch in one minute before starting time. That certainly doesn't impress the boss.

There's a better way.

The secret for success is to get to bed on time and to get up early. You've heard of Benjamin Franklin's saying: "Early to bed and early to rise makes a person healthy, wealthy and wise." You may hear Franklin's mantra quoted frequently because it's true.

Of course, going to bed earlier and waking up ear-lier so you can get to work early will require a change in your lifestyle. It may not be easy, but it will be worth the effort. Instead of staying up late to watch TV, record your favorite programs and watch them early the following evening. Don't schedule late social events on a work night.

Leave enough time in the morning (if you work the first shift) for a shower, a quiet breakfast and a tranquil drive to work. You will arrive early, refreshed, energized and ready to take on the day.

Key Ideas from Chapter 2

📁 You should never, ever arrive merely on time, or at the last minute, and you should definitely never arrive late. Instead, arrive at work at least a few minutes before starting time.

📁 Because the United States has a time-oriented culture, the start time of an event is very important. So, show respect to your employer by arriving early for work.

📁 Worrying about whether you are going to get paid for early arrival is being penny wise and dollar foolish.

📁 You may have to change your lifestyle in order to arrive to work early, but you will soon find these changes well worth the effort!

SECRET 3

Always Be Positive

SECRET 3:

Always Be Positive

President Ronald Reagan loved to tell a story about a young couple blessed with twin boys. As the boys grew up, it soon became apparent that even though they shared the same birthday, these siblings were as different as night and day. One was an eternal optimist and the other an invariable pessimist.

When the boys were seven years old, their parents decided to hire a psychiatrist to examine the twins and determine how they could be such polar opposites. First, the psychiatrist brought the pessimistic twin to a room. Opening the door, the psychiatrist showed the child a room overflowing with shiny new toys.

"All these toys are yours!" exclaimed the doctor. The little boy began to weep uncontrollably. "What on earth is wrong?" asked the psychiatrist.

Through his tears, the boy asked, "What am I going to do one day when they all begin to break?"

Then the psychiatrist took the optimistic twin to an old, dilapidated barn. He pushed opened the creaking door, revealing a heaping pile of manure covering the floor of the sagging old barn.

The little boy's eyes popped open wide, and his face lit up with a grin from ear to ear. He picked up a nearby shovel and began zealously scooping the manure.

"What in the world are you doing?" asked the baffled psychiatrist.

"Well," said the optimistic twin, "with all this manure, there must be a pony in here somewhere!"

No Complaining Allowed

When it comes to your job, your attitude has everything to do with your success or lack of it. Successful people are positive people. At first, you might think that they are positive because they are successful, but the truth is, they probably had a positive attitude long before they achieved success.

> *If you value your success,*
> *don't hang around with*
> *negative people.*

In fact, their positive attitude likely contributed to their success at work.

As you develop your positive attitude, remember that you must be positive *all* the time, not just some or even most of the time. Even if you're facing a task you don't particularly enjoy, you should accept it with a smile and attack it with gusto.

As a teenager on an egg ranch, I shoveled more chicken manure than I care to remember. It's not exactly something that you would ever choose to do. And I confess that we didn't always refer to it as "manure." But I learned that shoveling that stuff with a song in my heart was much better than grumbling the whole time.

It is especially important to be positive around fellow employees. And if you value your success, don't even hang around with negative people in the workplace. It's typical for people to gripe and complain about the job or about the management, but a grumbling spirit is quite contagious, so be on your guard against this plague and NEVER do it. The Bible warns against grumbling (cf. 1 Corinthians

10:10; James 5:9) and encourages us to "do every-thing without complaining or arguing" (Philippians 2:14). If someone around you starts grousing, be sure to either counter the comment with something positive or just walk away.

It's not wise to complain around your coworkers, because your grumbling WILL eventually get back to your supervisor. When it does, what do you think will happen to your raise? I sometimes wonder if negative people realize how often their promotions have been postponed, scaled back or cancelled because of remarks that got back to management.

Finally, if you should ever leave the organization, for whatever reason, do not say anything negative about it, no matter what. As a rule, never burn bridges in life, if you can help it at all.

The only thing worse than being late to work is being grumpy on the job. Like anybody else, your boss loves to have positive people around and loves to promote them!

But Most People Hate Their Jobs, Right?
You probably think I'm crazy with this talk about being positive on the job, because some surveys have indicated that nearly 90% of people hate their jobs! I can assure you that this dislike of the job shows up in the quality of their work. And then, is

> *You can choose to be part of the grumpy 90% or the successful 10%. It's up to you.*

it any wonder that most people aren't very successful in the workplace? The truth is you can choose to be part of the grumpy 90% or the successful 10%. It's up to you.

If you are part of the 90%, chances are that your superiors already perceive you as a negative person who is detrimental to their workforce. Your negativism will not only hold you back but also may be setting you up for a train wreck at work.

I once heard of a pastor who talked about what his wife called his "happy clothes." His happy clothes were the blue denim coveralls that he wore when he was working in his garden, his hobby. His wife called his coveralls his "happy clothes" because she noticed that he was much happier in his garden than in his workplace.

"Of course no one likes their job," the pastor proclaimed from the pulpit one Sunday. "Neither do I! I can't wait to get out of my office and slip into my happy clothes."

Granted, most people feel the way this pastor does.

But is this true for *you*? The positive 10%, those who know the secrets for success, have made their "happy clothes" their *work* clothes. What are *your* happy clothes?

Positive People Are Happier and Healthier

Have you noticed that positive people seem to always have smiles on their faces and that grumpy people always seem to wear frowns? The Bible says, "A happy heart makes the face cheerful" (Proverbs 15:13). Having a positive attitude is good for you because you will be happier not only on the job, but also at home and with other people.

Studies have shown that angry and negative people are actually at a greater risk for heart disease. When you are angry, your body releases chemicals that are harmful for your heart. According to Dr. James Welsh, "People who laugh actually live longer than those who are grumpy. Few realize that health actually varies according to the amount of laughter."

Proverbs 17:22 says, "A cheerful heart is good medicine." A positive attitude and lots of laughter will help keep you healthy and will help you heal if you get sick. In fact, many people believe that actor Christopher Reeve's improved physical state and relatively long life after his terrible accident were direct results of his extraordinarily positive attitude.

Be Positive about Criticism!

This may be the most difficult aspect to maintaining a positive attitude in the workplace. In fact, it might sound crazy that part of having a positive attitude is being positive about criticism and correction you receive from the boss! Yes, criticism can be difficult to swallow. We all prefer to have people praise us and applaud our efforts. However, we learn the most from criticism.

Instead of being defensive or angry about criticism you receive, welcome it! That's the best way for you to grow and become a better person. If you are negative and defensive about criticism, people will stop talking to you about where you can improve, and when this happens, you won't be able to grow.

When annual job evaluations come around, carefully look at the negative or less-than-stellar comments you receive. It is a natural tendency to overlook your faults and dwell on your perceived strengths, but listening to criticism will help you improve in areas that need work and will make you a more valuable employee.

An outstanding employee, one who knows the

secrets for success, will not leave the evaluation without asking for suggestions for improvement. Now that's being positive about criticism!

Become the Top Promoter

Be positive about your organization to everyone you meet, people inside and outside the organization. To be successful at your job, you ought to become the organization's top promoter and trumpet its praises everywhere. This means speaking a positive word about your workplace, its mission, the leadership and your coworkers whenever you get the opportunity.

Be sure also to support your organization *financially*. If you work at a store, be sure to shop there! Encourage your friends and family members to shop there as well. If your organization is sensitive to competitors, make sure you don't patronize the competition.

If you work for a non-profit organization that depends on donations, be sure to bless the organization with your generous financial support. Pass out brochures to your family, friends and people at church and ask them to support your organization as well.

Being a promoter makes you invaluable to the organization. I can guarantee your promoting of the workplace will not go unnoticed and will lead to your promotion *in* the workplace.

Being the top promoter does *not* mean that you should come across as "kissing up" to the boss. Do not become an annoyance to your fellow workers as if you are always looking for a pat on the head from management. Still, you can be a good influence on your fellow employees by modeling a positive and promoting spirit at all times.

Some of you might be reluctant to promote your organization. Perhaps because you don't really believe in its mission, or perhaps because you think you are already doing a lot for the organization simply by showing up every day.

It may be that your reluctance to promote your organization or company comes from some under-lying resentment or anger against the leadership in your workplace. Wilhelmus à Brakel, a Dutch theologian of the 17th century, points out that resentment or anger toward superiors may migrate into the arena of dishonoring those in authority over us.

In fact, dishonoring our superiors actually is a violation of the fifth commandment, "Honor your father and your mother" (Exodus 20:12). Brakel says people violate the fifth commandment "when

they *have no esteem* for their superiors, despising
them." In addition, "They sin when they are
*inwardly opposed to and have an aversion for their
superiors*" or when they "*mock* their superiors, or
ridicule them when they see their weaknesses."[6]

If you aren't willing or able to promote your place of
work, spend some time examining your motives.
You may find that you have legitimate reasons why
you can't promote the place where you work. If so,
it's probably time to find a new place to work.

Let Go of Your Balloon
To be positive all the time, you need to have an attitude of gratitude. The most common attitude for
people today is an entitlement attitude. If you have
an entitlement attitude or a victim attitude, you
will be a *whiner* rather than a *winner*.

An entitlement attitude says that the world owes
me a living because of my education, because of my
last name, because of my race or for any number of
other reasons. Sorry, but no one owes you anything.
It's time to stop whining and get to work!

A victim attitude is one that says, "I've been

wronged, so people should make it up to me some-
how." It is a variation on the entitlement attitude.
There may be times in your life when you have been
treated unjustly. Perhaps someone seriously sinned
against you. If so, part of healing from these hurts
should involve moving on and taking the initiative
to stop licking your wounds, and take control of
your life! I encourage you to adopt a humble attitude of forgiveness, recognizing that though you
may have been mistreated, others around you are
not required to give you special treatment.

Zacharias Ursinus was an author of the Heidelberg
Catechism, which was originally published in 1563.
Like Brakel, Ursinus saw implications for work in
the fifth commandment. For the 16th century theologian, "gratitude to superiors" is a must and it
"requires that everyone in his appropriate sphere
aid and promote the interest of those over him
according to his ability, and as occasion presents
itself."[7]

An entitlement attitude stems from self-involvement,
while an attitude of gratitude comes from selfless-
ness. Selfish people are more apt to have negative

attitudes about their jobs because they don't think they should have to work, for whatever reason. A successful person is grateful for the opportunity to go to work every day and make an honest living.

Indeed, attitude makes all the difference in the world. Imagine two people arriving for a job interview. Bob has a negative attitude. He comes in dreading the interview and expecting he will not get the job. He enters the room, shakes hands limply with the interviewer and looks to the floor. Right away he decides that the interviewer doesn't like him.

During the course of the interview, Bob speaks critically about the local sports team that is in last place, complains about the crummy weather, rails against our country "that is going to hell in a handbag" and says in no uncertain terms that his former employer gave him a raw deal. Bob is negative and is a whiner. Is Bob on the way to getting the job?

Bill interviews for the same job. Bill has an attitude of gratitude. He can't wait to get there and is early for the interview. He greets the interviewer with a smile and a firm handshake. He thanks her for the opportunity to meet with her. He knows no one owes him a living, but just picturing himself at that workplace excites him. During the interview, Bill tells the interviewer exactly why he thinks this is a great company and why he wants to work there. Bill is positive and is clearly a winner.

Would you hire Bob or Bill?

The secret is that a positive, grateful attitude is an essential component of the work ethic. The apostle Paul writes, "Give thanks in all circumstances, for this is God's will for you in Christ Jesus" (1 Thessalonians 5:18).

In his letter to the Philippians, Paul tells his readers, "Rejoice in the Lord always. I will say it again: Rejoice!" (Philippians 4:4). Have you ever wondered why Paul repeats himself here? A positive attitude must be very important, and it must be easy for someone or something to rob us of our joy.

A conference in Omaha, Nebraska distributed helium-filled balloons to attendees when they arrived. Participants were told to let the balloon go when they felt like expressing joy. At the end of the conference, a third of the people hadn't yet let go of their balloons.

Come on, it's time to let go of your balloon! Develop a positive attitude at work and everywhere else, and your success will soar like an eagle.

Key Ideas from Chapter 3

📁 Stay away from complaining on the job; your negative comments will be sure to get back to your employer. What's more, you should avoid hanging around with complainers in your workplace. They will only encourage a bad attitude and an atmosphere of discontent.

📁 Rather than being defensive about the criticism you receive on the job, welcome it! Most criticism will help you improve to become a better employee.

📁 Try to speak a positive word about your company or organization, its management and your supervisor whenever you get the opportunity.

📁 Become your employer's top promoter.

📁 An entitlement attitude on the job will put you on the road to failure. It's time to stop whining and get to work!

📁 A positive, grateful attitude is an essential component of the work ethic.

SECRET 4

Don't Be an Average Joe

SECRET 4:

Don't Be an Average Joe

You do not want to be an Average Joe in the work-place. You want always to do your job better than average. I've learned to try to give 110% in every-thing I do in life. When it comes to work, this means not only doing the job correctly, but also going the extra mile.

As a kid, this meant that if I was sweeping the concrete floor of the chicken building, I made sure I didn't miss any part, sweeping all the way into the corners and hanging the broom up when I was finished.

Giving 110% means *adding* to the job something that wasn't expected. When I was working at JCPenney while attending seminary, I would,

> *The employee handbook gives you all kinds of hints about how to give more than Average Joe.*

among other things, straighten up all the merchandise on the shelves of our department before I left for the night. It wasn't part of the job description, and I wasn't paid extra for doing so. But when I graduated and was leaving to continue my studies in Grand Rapids, Michigan, the management at JCPenney did its best to persuade me to stay and become a department manager.

You can always find something extra to do. All you have to do is keep your eyes open and be willing to give 110%.

Hints in the Handbook

Most workplaces have an employee handbook that contains all kinds of hints about how to give more than Average Joe. I suspect that many people don't even read the employee handbook (except to find out how much vacation time they get!). But, if you read the handbook and give 110% of what's expected, you'll quickly be on the path to success.

Some employees seem to think that they're doing pretty well if they adhere to 80% or 90% of the handbook guidelines. For example, some people do their job well but sometimes disregard aspects of the dress code. These people are sabotaging themselves and their careers. Ignoring the dress code, or any other part of the guidelines, negates a great amount of the good work they are doing.

Outstanding employees choose to follow all the rules, not just the ones they feel like following. And successful people are determined to follow the rules better than Average Joe does.

If the dress code is business casual, raise the bar to business sharp. If your job requires a particular performance quota, always exceed it. If you need to turn in your vacation requests six weeks in advance, submit yours ten weeks early. Instead of copying Average Joe and arriving at the last minute or showing up late, arrive at least ten minutes early to work.

When I say that Average Joe gives about 80%, I mean that he does just enough to get by. As I was discussing this with another employer, he said to me, "I wish I could get even 80% out of my workers!" His obvious frustration is why employers want their employees to know the secrets of success in the workplace.

Head and Shoulders above the Rest

Doing only as much as your employer expects of you, let alone doing less than is expected, is not enough. Can you imagine Michael Jordan giving only 80% or merely 100%? Michael Jordan would always arrive at practice first, work out more than anybody else and even come alone into the gym after a red-eye flight to shoot baskets for hours.

People have said that Michael Jordan was "a portrait of excess." As the legend himself says, "I don't do things half-heartedly. Because I know if I do, then I can expect half-hearted results." Jordan was no Average Joe.

Employers want to hire and promote people who work harder than Average Joe. A half-hearted effort will result in half-hearted results, while extraordinary effort will result in extraordinary results and your employer will notice the amount of effort you give.

Those who know what it takes to succeed in life give 110% or more. Their work is above average, and they stand head and shoulders above the rest. Giving 110% is a slam-dunk because bosses just love giving ambitious people raises and promotions!

It was mentioned at the outset that we find traces of the work ethic in Eastern religions. So, too, this idea of giving your all is present in other religions. Confucianism says, "Wherever you go, go with all your heart." In the Buddhist tradition it is said, "Your work is to discover your work and then with all your heart to give yourself to it." God has planted deep down in the heart of every man that he can aspire to something much greater than to be an Average Joe. And indeed you can!

Barriers to Giving 110%

Certain barriers will surely get in the way of giving 110%. If you want to succeed in the workplace and you find that one of these areas in your life is damaging your working habits, it may be time to make some adjustments.

Lack of Sleep: Lack of sleep will not only hinder your early arrival to work, it will also damage your performance all day long. Nothing is more discouraging for your boss than to hear Average Joe dragging his feet into the door whining, "Boy, I am SO tired! I didn't get to bed until after midnight last night!" Do you think this makes your boss feel sorry for him? When seeing a yawning employee, your boss isn't thinking, "Too bad Joe is so tired today.

> *In the same way God wired you for work, he also wired you for rest.*

Poor Joe." Here's what your boss is thinking: "Again Joe? You're SO unprepared for work. I'm obviously getting about 50% out of you today; shouldn't you receive only 50% of your pay for today?"

If you aren't getting enough sleep at night, you aren't going to be able to give 110% at work. Just like getting to work early, getting enough sleep may require a lifestyle change. Make some changes so you will be able to get adequate rest—your success depends on it!

Lack of a Sabbath's Rest: A Sabbath's rest is the Judeo-Christian belief that one day a week should be reserved for rest (a day for worship and no work). If you have a job that absolutely *requires* you to work on Sundays, then you ought to set aside another day for your Sabbath. Without a day of rest, you could even turn into a workaholic.

In the same way God wired you for work, he also wired you for rest. God designed us to rest one day in seven so we can give 110% during the workweek. Modeling this for us, God rested on the seventh day after the six days of creation. Genesis 2:2 tells us,

"God had finished the work he had been doing; so on the seventh day he rested from all his work." In fact, "God blessed the seventh day and made it holy, because on it he rested from all the work of creating that he had done" (Genesis 2:3). In Exodus 20, God's people are commanded to rest one day in seven because God did (20:11).

A second reason God's people are commanded to rest on the Sabbath is found in Deuteronomy 5:15:

> Remember that you were slaves in Egypt and that the Lord your God brought you out of there with a mighty hand and an outstretched arm. Therefore the Lord your God has commanded you to observe the Sabbath day.

Taking a Sabbath's rest shows that you are not a slave to your work and that you are grateful to rest in the finished work of God in Christ for you.

Average Joe, however, ignores all this and instead tires himself out on the day of rest with excessive recreation, "fun" activities, catching up on yard work and doing his own thing. He then arrives at work exhausted on Monday mornings and performs his job in his usual, average way, yawning and unfocused because he hasn't taken time to rest.

If you keep your feet from breaking the Sabbath, and from doing as you please on my holy day...and if you honor it by not going your own way and not doing as you please or speaking idle words, then you will find your joy in the Lord...(Isaiah 58:13-14).

Addictions: Although it may take some time before you notice the harmful effects of an addiction, few things can sabotage your success more. Obviously, your workday will be a failure if you arrive with a hangover, but any addiction (drugs, alcohol, gambling, sex, shopping, video gaming, etc.) will eventually tarnish your judgment, impair your job performance and harm relationships, not to speak of wasting away valuable time and draining your hard-earned money. You may cause permanent damage to your career before you even realize how thoroughly your addiction has taken over your life.

By definition, an addiction is something that enslaves you. If you are a slave to your addiction, it goes without saying that you will be unable to give 110% to your work. To be successful, you need to get rid of your addictions before they completely control you. Quit, see a doctor, attend a support group or enter rehab—do whatever it takes to get free, otherwise you will soon begin looking *worse* than Average Joe.

Failure to Follow Through: Giving 110% means finishing what you start. In fact, one of the most distinguishing characteristics of successful workers is their ability to "follow through." Successful people have a habit of finishing what they start, while people who fail to succeed in life have left in their wake a string of unfinished projects and unreached goals.

If you are a quitter, it will be very difficult for you to succeed on the job. You may make an impressive splash, but it will soon become evident that you will not make it to the finish line.

Follow-through is important for small projects during each day or larger projects that take several years to complete. Successful people, even if they are sick and tired of the project, are determined to bring it to completion.

Some people have all kinds of great ideas and are eager to implement them, but though these people begin projects, they never finish them. Each community has certain landmarks of failure to follow through: a half-painted business where the "newer" paint is already beginning to peel or a car perpetually on blocks in a neighbor's driveway. It's obvious that the implementers of these projects have no follow-through.

When you start a project on the job, be sure to see it to completion. In your personal life, become a person who finishes what you start. Whether it is a long-term or short-term project, only start what you will finish.

How do you know whether you will be able to finish a project? After all, everyone begins projects with lofty intentions. Before you start a project, "count the cost." This too is part of the work ethic. As Jesus says in Luke 14:28-30,

> Suppose one of you wants to build a tower. Will he not first sit down and estimate the cost to see if he has enough money to complete it? For if he lays the foundation and is not able to finish it, everyone who sees it will ridicule him, saying, "This fellow began to build and was not able to finish."

According to Jesus, quitters even become an object of scorn and ridicule. Because they fail to plan ahead, quitters waste precious time and resources; they are poor stewards and do not fulfill their role in the cultural mandate (see chapter 1). In contrast, faithful disciples plan ahead to make certain they

spend their God-given time and talents wisely.
Quitters never win, and winners never quit.

After you have counted the cost and determined
that a project is worthwhile, you must be persistent
in completing the project. In fact, financial expert
Dave Ramsey says, "Persistence is the number one
quality in successful people." Good employees not
only think of creative projects, they finish them!

We are all quitters by nature. Through Christ's
atonement for sin and in the power of the Holy
Spirit, we are empowered to make plans and, by
his grace, fulfill them. Sometimes God's plans are
not our plans, and we have to adjust our plans.
But a past littered with numerous unfinished
projects is more a sign of failure than of God's plan
surprising us.

Family Problems: Because family relationships
are the most important bonds you have in life, it is
imperative that you spend quality time investing in
your family. If there are problems in your marriage
or with your children, your mind will not be able to
focus on your work. Therefore, be sure to give your
marriage and your children the attention they
deserve. Study what it means to be a godly husband

> *If your success at work is not accompanied by success at home, your success will be bittersweet.*

or wife and an effective father or mother, and if a problem persists, be sure to get counseling before it's too late.

Make sure your drive to succeed at work is not causing problems at home. Your spouse and your children need time and attention from you. Make a conscious effort to make sure that you are not neglecting your family and thus adding to your family problems.

Even if you become successful at work despite family problems, you could be *more* successful if your home is in order. People who are successful at work but have problems in their families will never realize true success or fulfillment, because if your success at work is not accompanied by success at home, your success will be bittersweet.

Is all the success in the world really worth it if you come home one night to find your spouse's suitcases missing? Would workplace success be worth it if you received a phone call one day that one of your children had been arrested?

Resolving any problems with your spouse or your children will improve your life at home, and this is also essential to your success at work. Persistent family problems will plague your mind at work, and you will be unable to give 110%.

No family is perfect, many relationships go through times of conflict or tension and right now, you might be dealing with difficulties in your home. Correct those deficiencies to the best of your ability, starting with yourself. Average Joe will allow things to deteriorate at home while he attempts to be successful at work, but you should do more than Average Joe and concentrate on building a strong family in addition to working diligently.

Sluggards Need Not Apply

God didn't create men and women to be lazy, unproductive couch potatoes. The Bible often speaks about lazy people and laziness in unflattering terms.

This why the apostle Paul says, "If a man will not work, he shall not eat" (2 Thessalonians 3:10). Commenting on this passage, John Calvin, the father of the work ethic, says, "Paul censures those lazy drones who lived by the sweat of others, while they contribute no service in common for aiding the human race."[8]

Likewise, the book of Proverbs pokes fun at the sluggard who lies in bed all day (cf. Proverbs 6:9-11; 26:13-15). "As a door turns on its hinges, so a sluggard turns on his bed" (Proverbs 26:14).

Wilhelmus à Brakel uses strong language when he writes that laziness is *theft* and then lists various other facts about laziness:[9]

- *A sluggard is abominable to everyone*—"as vinegar to the teeth, and as smoke to the eyes" (Proverbs 10:26). [In other words, lazy people are just plain irritating to have around. They are a nuisance and seem to get in the way of productive society.]

- *A sluggard is a fit instrument for the devil*—an accomplice to the devil (1 Timothy 5:12-15). [In this passage, the author censures lazy home-makers and others who waste time they should spend working. He points out that they are nothing more than idlers, gossips and busy-bodies who, as they waste time and waste words, become Satan's workers.]

- *A sluggard is a burden to himself*—and his way "is blocked with thorns" (Proverbs 15:19). [Lazy people always seem to have thorny "problems" blocking their progress on the road of life. They have a knack for turning molehills into mountains, and they always have a "crisis of the day." In this way, sluggards are their own worst enemies.]

- *A sluggard makes himself poor*—(Proverbs 6:9-11). [Not all poverty can be blamed on laziness. However, all laziness will certainly lead to poverty—of finances and/or of spirit. In this sense, lazy people are at fault for their poverty.]

- *Laziness engenders fornication and theft.* [It is interesting that this last reason is the only one for which Brakel provides no biblical reference. We can assume that Brakel considered the point so obvious that it required no further support!]

The Bible is not the only religious source condemning laziness. A Nigerian proverb picks up on this important theme when it says, "Weeping is not the answer to poverty; a lazy man who is hungry has no one to blame but himself." Similarly, Mahatma Gandhi remarked, "Purity of mind and idleness are incompatible." And Benjamin Franklin, a deist, maintained that "idleness and pride tax with a heavier hand than kings and governments."

You might object to all this talk about sluggards, thinking, "Hey, but Average Joe isn't lazy. He shows up and does the job. Sure, Average Joe's work isn't A+, but he gets the job done." However, Average Joe is walking too close to the line of laziness, occasionally or even regularly drifting over the edge. To be successful, you should make sure you stay *as far as possible* from the edge. Give 110% just to be sure! Surely your boss has more than enough Average Joes with whom to deal every day.

Why We Give 110%

Ultimately, pleasing our employers and achieving the next promotion are not the reasons we give 110%. We work hard because it is part of the work ethic.

In Luke 17:7-10, Jesus tells a parable about a servant who worked all day doing what his master required. The servant spent the day plowing the field or watching the sheep and later that evening prepared supper and served his master before preparing a meal for himself. Jesus asks his disciples, "Would [the master] thank the servant because he did what he was told to do?" (vs. 9).

The implied answer is, "Of course not." Jesus concludes, "So you also, when you have done everything you were told to do, should say, 'We are unworthy servants; we have only done our duty'" (vs. 10). Likewise, you should not expect a pat on the back for simply doing your duty.

John Calvin says God has "a right to demand the services of our whole life, to the utmost extent that our ability allows, and yet be in no degree indebted to us."[10] Why wouldn't we expect every person of faith to give 110%?

Confucianism evokes the Golden Rule when it comes to giving our best where it says, "When you are laboring for others, let it be with the same zeal as if it were for yourself." The Bible ups the ante when Paul says we are to work with joy in everything we do because in the end, our real boss is *the Lord* (cf. Colossians 3:22-24; Ephesians 6:5-8). Since Christ has forgiven us and called us his friends, what more incentive do we need to work wholeheartedly for his glory?

So, you want to succeed in the workplace? Here's the secret: don't be someone who just gets by. It is not adequate to be good, or even very good, at your job. Those who succeed give more, much more, than Average Joe does. They always go the extra mile on the road to success.

Key Ideas from Chapter 4

📁 Always give 110% on the job, and you will be an invaluable employee who stands out above the rest.

📁 Lack of sleep will not only hinder your early arrival to work, it will also damage your performance all day long.

📁 God designed us to rest one day in seven so we can give 110% during the workweek.

📁 To be successful, you need to get rid of your addictions before they control you.

📁 Successful people have "follow-through," the habit of finishing what they start.

📁 Be sure to give your family members the attention they deserve.

📁 Everyone is expected to work, and God hates laziness. So, don't expect a pat on the back for simply doing your job.

SECRET 5

Don't Bounce Around

SECRET 5:

Don't Bounce Around

As an employer, I've received thousands of job applications over the years. Some are obviously more impressive than others, but I always raise my eyebrows when I receive a cover letter reading something like, "I believe I am a perfect fit for the job. As you can see in my resume, I have a LOT of experience." Usually the resume following a statement like that reveals an applicant who has had ten jobs in about as many years.

Does that person really have a LOT of experience?

Lots of Jobs, Little Experience

In reality, bouncing around from job to job creates a worker with very little experience. People who bounce around may have a year of experience doing

> *A person who has been bouncing around looks like someone who has problems on the job.*

a myriad of things, but they have never mastered any one skill, let alone gained real experience on the job.

Job jumpers might be able to get entry-level positions at dead-end jobs, but they have great difficulty landing the really good positions. Why? Because a person who has been bouncing around looks like someone who is an opportunist or who has problems on the job, someone eager to abandon ship for the slightest of reasons or raises.

Think about it: why would an organization spend time and effort to train a worker for an important position if that person's history suggests a short stay?

Employers are looking for people whose work history shows they will be dedicated to their job and to the organization. They seek to hire people who have already gained valuable knowledge and will be able to contribute to the organization.

Pay Your Dues
When you first enter the workforce, you will probably start off in a low-paying (perhaps minimum

wage), entry-level job. Never be too proud to start at a lowly position (cf. Philippians 2:5-7). You must pay your dues.

According to the *Cambridge International Dictionary of Idioms*, "to pay your dues" means "to work hard or do something unpleasant over a long period in order to achieve something."[11] The phrase is based on the literal meaning of the word "dues," which is money paid to belong to an organization.

Let's break it down. To pay your dues means:

- *To work hard or do something unpleasant—* It's doing a nasty job few people would do.

- *To do it over a long period of time*—Anyone can endure a nasty job for a short time, but enduring it for a long time requires discipline and sacrifice.

- *To do it in order to achieve something*—It's denying yourself immediate gratification in order to achieve long-term satisfaction.

In other words, belonging to the elite club of the successful will cost you. You will have to pay the price.

My son-in-law, Joel, owns a concrete pouring business. It is brutally difficult, backbreaking work. On the job, Joel and his brothers take lunch at noon but refuse any other breaks during the day. Few can go the distance with these tigers.

One day, a brand new employee began his first day working with Joel. He worked through the morning, left for lunch and never returned for the afternoon shift. In fact, they never saw or heard from him again! He wasn't willing to work that hard. He wasn't willing to pay his dues.

My wife, our four children and I all paid our dues in the workplace. I've told you about the years I spent shoveling tons of chicken manure, and that's not even half the story of that distasteful job on the egg ranch. As a young girl, my wife almost passed out in the blazing sun while she picked blueberries, strawberries and asparagus—jobs that most folks today simply refuse to do.

Our children learned the work ethic when they were young, doing chores inside and outside the house. As they grew up, each of them paid their dues, working hard in low-paying jobs: Greg in a plant nursery, Lisa in a deli, Rebecca as an aid in a nursing home and Tim as a bagboy.

The point is, everyone should be willing to pay their dues and start at the bottom. Do not be too proud to do the lowliest of tasks and cheerfully do your work wherever God has placed you.

> *Don't give up too easily or too early; you might quit when success is just around the corner.*

No matter what, stick with it! Bloom where you're planted and work your way up. Don't give up too easily or too early; you might quit when success is just around the corner. If you follow the secrets in this book, I can guarantee that you won't spend the rest of your life in entry-level positions.

After a time, if you are honestly under-appreciated at work and you are not getting ahead or moving up the way you should according to the quality of your work, you will have paid your dues and earned the right to look for a new job somewhere else. By this point, you will have some real experience to recommend you for something better.

Temptations to Bounce

Not bouncing around is actually more difficult than it sounds. You might think that once you have found a job you really like it will be easy to stick with it. In reality, though, there are many reasons people are tempted to bounce from job to job, no matter what the job is. Let's take a look at some of these reasons.

> *A habit of leaving jobs
> for others that promise
> to pay more shows
> discontentment.*

Higher Pay: You can usually find a job that pays more than the job you have right now. However, you should not consider changing jobs for pay unless the offer is so significant and the dream position appears so perfect for you that it is absolutely irresistible. The problem is that people are easily "bought off" and tend to leave for relatively slight increases in pay that will never pay off in the long run.

A habit of leaving jobs merely for more money may indicate discontentment. Christians are called to find contentment in Christ, not in material things. Paul says, "I have learned to be content whatever the circumstances" (Philippians 4:11), and we too ought to learn to be content, even if we are "paying our dues" in an undesirable position. In 1 Timothy 6:6, Paul tells Timothy, "Godliness with contentment is great gain."

It is true the Bible also teaches that "the worker deserves his wages" (1 Timothy 5:18). There is nothing wrong with making all you can in life and working hard to earn a new position. John Wesley famously said, "Make all you can, save all you can, give all you can!" However, in the long run, bouncing around to different jobs will not make you the most money. And if you are having financial problems, I can assure you that a higher paying "quick fix" will not help you. Instead you may find that financial counseling is needed to establish better habits for handling your money, regardless of how much you make.

Remember, it is better for your *long-term value* in the workplace to stick with your current position, even at a lower pay rate for now, than to risk jeopardizing your career by building a resume of short stays and thus looking opportunistic or unreliable. If you stick with your job and follow the secrets, especially giving 110% at work, it is likely that soon enough you will get a raise, and in the meantime you will have developed many valuable skills.

Not What You Expected: It happens. Once you get into the job, you find that your position or your work environment is not what you expected. Suddenly things aren't looking so good. When you accepted this job, you were jumping up and down with excitement, but now that you have started working, you realize that this job isn't quite as exciting as you had thought it would be.

If you find yourself in this disappointing position, I encourage you to stick with it. You may learn to enjoy this job, or it may lead to some other position in the company where you can flourish. In time, you may be pleasantly surprised by the unexpected.

The bottom line is that if you sensed God was leading you to accept this position, there may be things he wants to teach you here, even if at first you can't see them. Learn what you can from this job, put the seven secrets into practice and you will find that you will discover fulfillment and success at work—either in this job or in the next.

Conflict: If at first your job seems to be exactly what you were expecting, you're probably in the "honeymoon stage." During this time you may believe you have finally found the perfect job, with great coworkers and even the perfect boss. You may think to yourself, "Is this possible? This job is perfect for me—even better than I expected!"

Now I don't want to be discouraging, but the truth is that your job isn't going to seem *perfect* forever. The honeymoon usually lasts six months to a year, but can be as short as a few weeks or as long as a few years. No matter how long your honeymoon stage lasts, inevitably there will be a "conflict stage"

when things start to look less promising. The disap-
pointment usually centers on job relationships (with
the boss and/or fellow employees), and this may
leave you confused because at first this seemed to
be the perfect job.

In the conflict stage, relationships are tested. Every
relationship—your job, your marriage and other
relationships—will have a conflict stage. The honeymoon can't last forever, and when conflict comes,
many will simply bail out. Of course, if you bail out
here, you will have to face the same stages all over
again in a new position.

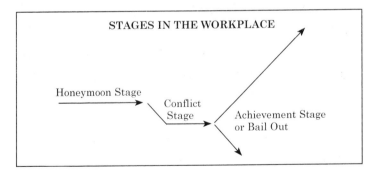

However, if you patiently resolve the relationship
tensions, you can advance to the "achievement
stage." At this stage, relationships are strength-

ened, forged in the fire of testing. You can achieve exciting things with these new and tested relationships. You will enjoy your work more than ever, and you will be firmly on the road to success.

Working the System: There are those who bounce around because they have learned to "milk the system." By that we mean, of course, those who start out at a new position in a government or for-profit company but have no intention of staying long term. In fact, they count on getting fired or "hurt" so they can attempt to claim unemployment or disability income. Many will try to collect even if they were not fired or "hurt," but simply quit on their own accord. They will work at a job just long enough to qualify for assistance.

These bottom-feeders of society may think they are outsmarting the system as they receive checks for doing nothing, but they are actually sabotaging themselves. They will never achieve true success in life because they settle for income far below their true earning potential. Rather than contributing to making this world a better place, they become a drain on society. To make matters worse, they train their children to sap off others, creating future generations of sluggards.

Certainly society must have a temporary safety net in place for those who are unexpectedly laid off from their jobs and for those who are genuinely disabled. However, if you have a resume with numerous short stays and "accidents" on the job, you may cause future potential employers to wonder whether you are working the system as you bounce around.

How Long Is Long Enough?
So, how long should you stay at your job? Ideally, you should give an organization at least five years. If your stay is shorter than three years and you leave without good reason, future potential employers may wonder what went wrong, and they will probably think it was your fault.

How does "sticking with it" fit into the work ethic? First, we certainly believe God leads people in their lives. God can lead you to a new job, but I doubt he would change his mind every year! So job jumping is *not* following God's leading in your life.

Second, Christians should be known by qualities such as faithfulness, loyalty, dependability, content-ment, perseverance, patience and maturity (cf. Galatians 5:22-23; Colossians 3:12; 2 Peter 1:6). It is difficult to imagine a person with these qualities bouncing around from job to job. In a strictly moral sense, longevity says something about character. Job jumpers may think they have a drive to succeed, but in reality, they are on the road to career failure.

According to the experts, most folks don't find their *long-term* fit until their mid-forties. Of course, some people will be fortunate enough to find it right away, but since most don't, you probably will change jobs from time to time.

But the key word here is "time"; give it some time. You limit your opportunities for finding that excellent long-term fit if you bounce around frequently. Stick around and get some real experience for your resume!

Key Ideas from Chapter 5

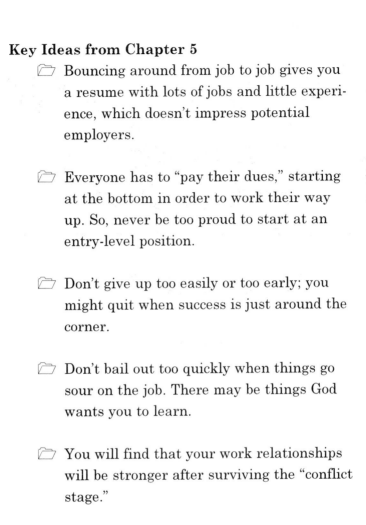

- Bouncing around from job to job gives you a resume with lots of jobs and little experience, which doesn't impress potential employers.

- Everyone has to "pay their dues," starting at the bottom in order to work their way up. So, never be too proud to start at an entry-level position.

- Don't give up too easily or too early; you might quit when success is just around the corner.

- Don't bail out too quickly when things go sour on the job. There may be things God wants you to learn.

- You will find that your work relationships will be stronger after surviving the "conflict stage."

- Those who work the system may think they are outsmarting the system as they receive checks for doing nothing, but they are actually sabotaging themselves.

SECRET 6

Become a Change Agent

SECRET 6:

Become a Change Agent

A newly married husband was watching his bride prepare a ham for dinner. He noticed she cut off both ends of the ham before she put it in the pan. Perplexed, the husband asked, "Sweetie, why did you cut off the ends of the ham before you put it in the pan?"

"I don't know," confessed his wife. "That's the way my mother has always done it."

The next time they were having dinner at the in-laws' he was eager to get to the bottom of the mystery. "Mom," he asked, "why do you cut off both ends of the ham before you cook it?"

> *Becoming a change agent is probably the hardest secret to put into practice.*

"I don't know," said his mother-in-law. "I guess that's the way my mother always did it."

Now the man was even more determined. The next time he and his wife visited Grandma in the rest home, he probed a bit. "Grandma, why did you always cut off both ends of the ham before you cooked it?"

"Well, my pan was too small," she said.

Change Resisters vs. Change Agents

Just like the new bride in the story, most people try to avoid change. Always doing things the same way is the path of least resistance. For this reason, becoming a change agent is not easy. It takes a lot of work to become a change agent—more work than any of the other secrets require. Although it is difficult to discipline yourself to get to bed on time so you can arrive at work early, and it might feel tiring to always give 110%, becoming a change agent will most likely be the hardest secret to put into practice.

Becoming a change agent requires a paradigm shift. To move from resisting change to being a change agent, you must change your entire orientation. And although this secret may be difficult to implement, becoming a change agent will bring the most fulfillment and satisfaction to your work and life.

There is a tendency for Average Joe to resist change on the job. When management introduces something new, he groans. For him, change is a nuisance; it means more effort for him while the organization gets used to the change. Average Joe digs in his heels and is "change resistant." It never occurs to him to ask, "Why do we cut off the ends of the ham?" because it's easier to do things the way they've always been done.

On the other hand, change agents gladly accommodate change. They get excited about new challenges and welcome change like a fresh breeze. For them, change is good. In fact, change agents are always considering how to do things better and (with utmost diplomacy) even make suggestions for change. Change agents are the ones who ask, "Why do we cut off the ends of the ham?"

It's important to note that this secret requires being a change agent according to your boss' agenda, not

If you have habits that don't line up with the secrets in this book, change those habits!

your own. Discover where *your boss* wants to take the company and do everything in your power to help him get it there.

Good Habits vs. Bad Habits

People tend to be creatures of habit, and often following habits is easier than putting forth the effort to change and learn a new way.

The good news is, you don't have to change *all* your habits. In fact, some habits can be good. For instance, when it comes to work, *always* arriving early, *always* being positive, *always* giving 110% and *always* being dependable are habits that lead to success on the job. Never change those habits!

However, while maintaining those habits, it is likely that you have some bad habits you ought to change. You need to be willing to let go of these habits to change and grow along with your organization.

If you have habits that are diminishing your productivity or encouraging your coworkers to diminish their productivity, change those habits! If you have habits that don't line up with the secrets in this book, change those habits! If you have habits that are in any way holding your organization back, change those habits!

Top employees know that successful organizations are always changing. As organizations grow, excellent workers constantly search for better ways to do things. Employers are looking for people with good habits. But successful organizations also need people who can change other habits to grow with the organization.

How to Become a Change Agent

At this point you may be wondering how you can become a change agent. How do you get off the dead-end path of change resistance?

While there isn't a magic formula, becoming a change agent in the workplace requires that you work to adapt your feelings, thoughts and actions with respect to change.

Change Your Attitude: Becoming a change agent starts with a change of attitude. Hopefully, since you've already read chapter 3, "Always Be Positive," you already are working to develop a positive attitude in the workplace. If so, I'm sure that your glass looks half full instead of half empty.

Attitude has to do with our feelings or dispositions toward certain situations, things or persons. Just as we need to think positively about our jobs, co-workers and bosses, we also need to learn to have a positive attitude about *change*. Some of us naturally see change as a bad thing, so learning to look positively upon change requires a 180-degree adjustment of attitude.

Change Your Thinking: Becoming a change agent also requires a shift in your thinking. To change any attitude or habit, you need to become willing to consider different options and to look at things from a new point of view.

The Apostle Paul talks about a Christian's need to be "transformed by the renewing of your mind" (Romans 12:2). This happens at conversion and needs to continue to happen throughout our lives. Alcoholics Anonymous recognizes the need for a new thinking in order to change bad habits. They refer to the old thinking as "stinking thinking."

Working as change agents, many great inventors throughout history had to think outside the box. Whether it was the Wright brothers thinking about flight in a new way, Albert Einstein's overturning of the principles of Newtonian physics or Thomas Edison's prolific inventing, they all succeeded as change agents because they thought differently than others.

Your job may not involve inventing, but every job involves being *inventive*. And while most of us aren't going to come up with new ideas that will change world history, we all can help to make improvements in our organizations. So, if you want to accomplish great things on the job, you too need to think differently. You will be amazed to find that you have a fresh perspective on the world around you, including your workplace.

Critical to thinking in new ways is a *formal education*. In the middle of the 20th century, career success usually required a high school diploma. In the 21st century, however, the minimum of a college degree is necessary.

Without a high school diploma or GED, you may qualify for minimum wage jobs, but be aware that unemployment lines are overflowing with high school dropouts. And the glass ceiling on your career will be painfully low.

However, today, finishing high school usually falls short of what you need for long-term success in the workplace. Without a college degree or some kind of very specialized training, it will be difficult for you to get past entry-level jobs, and next to impossible to ever land a really good position.

You may well be able to slip into an excellent

organization without a college degree, but you won't be able to get very far before you hit a brick wall due to your lack of education. The fact is that on average, college graduates earn more and climb higher in the workforce than those who discontinue their formal education.

So, if you dropped out of high school, you need to complete your GED. If you are already in the work-force but do not have a college degree, start taking a course or two on the side until you finish. Make sure taking courses doesn't negatively affect the quality of your work in your day job or your drive for more education will be self-defeating.

If earning a bachelor's degree sounds too daunting, start with earning a two-year degree (A.A.) and then go to work on finishing the next two years of a degree program (B.A. or B.S.). Of course, if you can eventually go further, all the better.

Why are people with a formal education more suc-cessful in the workplace? Besides the fact that their degree demonstrates they work hard to achieve something of significance, *a good education teaches you how to think*. It teaches you to think in new ways as you are exposed to new ideas, challenging both your conceptions and your misconceptions.

Higher education equips you with the language and

the communication tools necessary to express your-self in a clear and compelling way. In addition, a college education will give you a broad knowledge base from which to draw in the future and the research and study skills required for a lifetime of learning and growing.

In other words, a good education awards you with an open mind. People without a college education are often resistant to change and close-minded. In fact, many do not pursue a college education because they are fearful or suspicious of education, knowing that it would challenge their thinking. Because productive companies and organizations do not want fearful and close-minded employees, it's easy for human resource departments with hun-dreds of resumes piled on a desk to dump those without an impressive educational history.

Give Yourself New Experiences: In addition to a formal education, you need to continue to learn informally. Any new experience can help you to think differently about the way you live. However, if you have the opportunity to travel, immersing yourself in another culture may be the best way to develop the skills of a change agent. When you live in a different culture, you have no choice but to see EVERYTHING in a new way.

My family lived in the Netherlands for almost three

years while I attended school there. My wife and I enrolled our kids in the Dutch schools where they had to sink or swim. My wife had to learn the language so she could talk with the neighbors and get her shopping done. I needed to learn the language so that I could understand my professors!

However, our everyday experiences were as educational as any formal education. Changes in our thinking went far beyond the fact that a "chair" was now a "stoel" and a "store" was now a "winkel." The people around us introduced us to a number of new ways to think about everyday activities.

For example, we experienced a new way to bid farewell. When you leave a Dutch home, the Dutch will stand outside the door and say "goodbye" in a dozen different ways, continuously waving and saying goodbye until you are in your car or on your bike, out of the driveway and *completely* out of sight. Only when you are out of sight will they step back into their home.

Not so in America (at least everywhere I've lived). Here when you leave a family's home, most times they will be back in their house, with the door slammed shut and porch lights out, practically before you even get your car started! Before we moved to the Netherlands, this is what we were used to doing. But after living in the Netherlands, we experienced a change in our thinking and practice, and now the American practice seems rude to us.

Even if it's not practical to experience another culture, let me suggest some ways you can give yourself new learning experiences that aren't as drastic as packing up and moving to a new country:

- Take *brief* trips to different places near and far, as you are able. In the global village, the world is at our doorstep. It is likely that there are a number of cultures represented in areas not too far away from where you live. Seek out those places and immerse yourself in a new culture.

- Read or listen to books on topics that are new to you and or with which you initially might disagree. Use the Internet to follow a newspaper from a different country. When you watch TV, choose educational channels such as PBS, the Discovery Channel, the History Channel and the Science Channel. In this way, you can expose yourself to new cultures, stories and ways of thinking right in your own home!

- Learn a foreign language. Thinking about different ways to talk about something will lead you to different ways of thinking about things. Ideally, other languages were part of your formal education. But you can also learn much on your own. As you learn the language, take time to learn about the cultures that speak it.

- Make a point of befriending people who are quite different from you in terms of culture, ethnicity, interests, ideology and even religion. Get to know your neighbor down the street who has always seemed "different." Volunteer to provide a service in your community; chances are good that you will serve alongside someone who is different from you. As you make new friends and meet new people, learn from them and try to understand their way of living life.

Provide as many varied experiences as possible for yourself and your family. This may seem frightening at first—we would much rather be in places where we are comfortable. But the best way to shift your paradigm is to expose yourself to new, strange and wonderful things. And nothing less than a paradigm shift is required to accomplish the sometimes daunting task of becoming a change agent.

Comfort in God's Unfolding Plan
Becoming a change agent isn't easy because change can be downright daunting at times. This paradigm shift will be impossible *unless* you no longer find comfort in tradition and instead find your only comfort in Jesus Christ who is "the same yesterday and today and forever" (Hebrews 13:8).

In Christ we find the only true source of comfort and perfect stability. John Calvin explains Hebrews 13:8 in this way:

> This then is a remarkable passage, from which we learn that there is no other way of being truly wise than by fixing all our thoughts on Christ alone.[12]

God's truth is unchanging, but the times in which we apply those truths change constantly. We can make those changes best if Christ is our firm foundation. God is not standing still as he unfolds his plan of redemption from one generation to the next. We must be ready and willing to change as he changes us with mercies that are new every morning (Lamentations 3:23).

If you make the paradigm shift from being change resistant to becoming a change agent, you might be surprised to see that your salary will change too, and that's a change anyone can welcome!

Key Ideas from Chapter 6

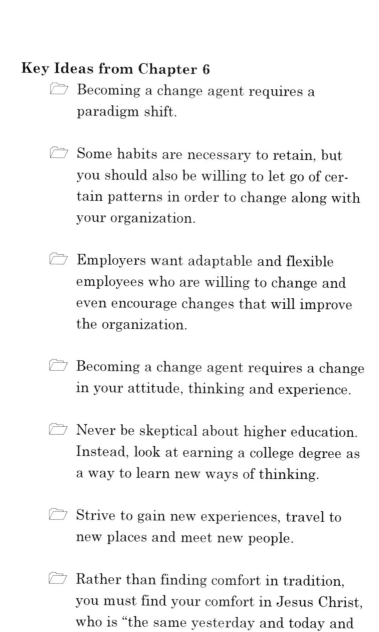

- 🗁 Becoming a change agent requires a paradigm shift.

- 🗁 Some habits are necessary to retain, but you should also be willing to let go of certain patterns in order to change along with your organization.

- 🗁 Employers want adaptable and flexible employees who are willing to change and even encourage changes that will improve the organization.

- 🗁 Becoming a change agent requires a change in your attitude, thinking and experience.

- 🗁 Never be skeptical about higher education. Instead, look at earning a college degree as a way to learn new ways of thinking.

- 🗁 Strive to gain new experiences, travel to new places and meet new people.

- 🗁 Rather than finding comfort in tradition, you must find your comfort in Jesus Christ, who is "the same yesterday and today and forever."

SECRET 7

Find a Mentor

SECRET 7:

Find a Mentor

Regardless of age or experience, everyone can benefit from the support and advice of another. A mentor is a person with more experience than you, someone a few steps ahead of you on the road of life, someone who can become your coach and your confidant.

When I first became a minister, my church denomination decided to begin a mentoring program where new pastors would be assigned to older pastors who would show them the ropes. I was surprised at the program because I had a mentor; in fact, he had already been my mentor for many years. "Doesn't everyone have a mentor?" I wondered.

Somewhat perplexed, I called the denominational office to ask why they thought they needed this program. They claimed that my situation, already having a mentor when I began my ministry, was extremely unusual. Most new pastors (at that time, at least) were going it alone. The denomination knew that having a mentor is crucial to a person's success and therefore wanted to make sure all new ministers had this opportunity.

A mentor, someone who has already done what you're doing, will be able to guide you and help you quickly learn how to succeed at your job.

My Mentor

When I was a young man in the business world, my dad was my mentor. But when I went into ministry, it would have been quite a stretch for him to understand my new world, and it would have been very difficult for him to guide me though this stage of my life.

That's why, when I was in college, I found "Doc." Throughout our mentoring relationship, Dr. Alexander De Jong was always the kind of person that I could call anytime with any question. After college, we no longer lived near each other, but we maintained our relationship mainly by telephone.

I'll never forget one Sunday in my first pastorate

when my mentor bailed me out of a difficult situation. About an hour before the start of the worship service, I was sitting in my office, still very unhappy with my sermon, which had refused to come together during the week. In my distress, I called my mentor, Doc. He gave me some advice based on his own experiences. I hit a home run with that sermon, thanks to my mentor pulling me from the ditch.

Of course, his regular mentoring came in handy for more than sermon crises. He guided me through a host of other situations, from tough counseling situations to handling difficult people to church program strategies.

I think the most helpful part of our mentoring relationship was that Doc accepted me unconditionally and had 100% confidence in me. This in turn reassured me that I could really open up to him.

Your Mentor

You need a mentor, no matter what kind of work you are doing. You may think your job is not important enough to need a mentor, but everyone will do better in life under a good mentor. A person with whom you have a strong relationship could be your mentor, or you could have more than one mentor, each with special expertise for a particular area of your life.

> *Good mentors are open
> enough to counsel you
> out of their successes
> and their failures.*

Good mentors are open enough to counsel you out
of their successes *and* their failures. Be cautious
about a "mentor" who only talks about accomplish-
ments. People should learn the most from their mistakes, and you can learn much from your mentor's
mistakes.

Mentors who can share wisdom from their successes
as well as their failures are invaluable because they
can help you avoid unnecessary mishaps. If you
take time to learn from your mentor, you can avoid
unnecessary mistakes in your life. This is a certain
way to get on the fast track to success.

Biblical Models for Mentorship

Having a mentor is an important part of the work
ethic. At first you might balk at the claim that
having a mentor is an ethical or moral issue. However, part of the work ethic is doing your best. You
owe it to your job, to your community and to God to
do everything to the best of your ability. So, if
having a mentor makes you a more effective
worker, and a better person, don't you have an ethical, moral responsibility to find a mentor?

Besides, God gave us examples of mentoring relationships in Scripture. When Jesus was on this earth, he had 12 disciples. This was not unusual in itself. In Bible days, a rabbi or teacher had followers who learned from a person they called their "teacher," or even their "master."

Rabbis were deeply respected mentors. Rooted firmly in the Torah, they were men of wisdom and understanding. But they were responsible to pass on more than "head knowledge" to their students. Because a rabbi's disciples followed his every move, they learned "heart knowledge" from his example of devout living.

Jesus had an especially close mentoring relationship with three of his disciples, Peter, James and John. These three men were some of the first chosen in the list of disciples (Matthew 10:2), and Jesus included them in special mentoring sessions (cf. Mark 5:37). Jesus took them up to the Mount of Transfiguration where they were able to witness his glory displayed (Matthew 17:1). The Savior even shared with them the most personal and intense struggle of his life—his profound agony in the Garden of Gethsemane (Mark 14:33).

You may wonder why these three disciples received "special" treatment over the other nine. The fact is that all mentoring occurs in ever-expanding circles of influence. Besides the 12, there were others who followed Jesus closely, such as Mary Magdalene, Martha and Lazarus. In fact, there were hundreds and even thousands who followed him, listening to him teach and experiencing his healing.

But Jesus reserved a special, intense mentoring relationship for only three. If someone is willing to be your mentor at that level, that person is making you a priority, and if the relationship is right, you should be deeply grateful. By the same token, if you find someone who is only able to give you second or third tier attention, be grateful for that as well, and supplement the wisdom you gain there with that of others who can help you.

Biblical models for mentorship do not begin and end with Jesus. For example, in the Old Testament, we have the example of Elijah and Elisha. Later, in the New Testament, the Apostle Paul mentored many churches. He had a special relationship with some of those churches, such as the church in Philippi. And we know that Paul personally mentored Timothy and Titus, young pastors who looked to him for guidance, in an especially intimate way. He even referred to Timothy as his "true son" (cf. 1 Timothy 1:2).

Mentoring is not only for ministry, of course. All life is sacred and every sphere of life belongs to God's kingdom. He intends to use mentors to guide you

Keep your eyes open and look for a person you would like to emulate.

through life. First and foremost, Jesus ought to be your mentor. In addition, great leaders of the past can mentor us through the writings they have left behind.

But ultimately, God designed us to have face-to-face mentors on earth to guide us in a personal way. This is also recognized in Buddhism, which says, "Follow, then, the shining ones, the wise, the awakened, the loving, for they know how to work and forbear."

Hopefully this begins with our parents. And then it can grow and expand to other significant people who are a few steps ahead of us in life.

So Where Do You Find One?

Where do you find that mentor? Most importantly, keep your eyes open and look for a person you would like to emulate. I started coming to Dr. De Jong's church to hear him preach and eventually took classes he taught at Trinity Christian College. After class, I would strike up conversations with him and ask him questions. I thought to myself, "Someday I want to preach like him, and I'd like to be that kind of person, by God's grace." He eventually took me under his wing. You can't *force* a mentoring relationship with someone. Sometimes it "clicks" and sometimes it doesn't.

Your mentor may be a family member or someone you know from church. It helps if your mentor is in the same line of work as you or a line of work that is related to what you hope to do.

You may even find a mentor on the job. For instance, you may have a manager or boss who is willing to serve as your mentor, or you may be part of a formally-arranged career mentorship called an apprenticeship. However, a mentoring relationship doesn't have to be formalized and spelled out in detail to be effective. It could just develop naturally on its own.

Ultimately, a mentor should be someone you respect and would like to follow. In the same way, your mentor should be willing and able to lead and counsel you. In a mentoring relationship, both the student and the mentor understand the level of involvement expected in the relationship—second or third tier level of attention or that special, intense, intimate relationship.

Key Ideas from Chapter 7

☐ A mentor is someone a few steps ahead of you on the road of life and someone who can become your coach and confidant.

☐ Seek out a mentor in your field of employment who can help you by sharing from his/her successes *and* failures.

☐ Since having a mentor makes you a more effective worker, and a better person, you have an ethical, moral responsibility to find one (or more).

☐ Mentoring occurs in ever-expanding circles of influence.

☐ Your mentor should be someone you respect and would like to follow.

*No one is perfect,
and you have made
and will make mistakes.
Don't throw up your
hands and despair...*

EPILOGUE

It is no secret that the disparity between the wealthy and the working poor increases every year. Many experts have devoted their studies to discovering the reasons for this growing disparity, but in the meantime, the rich still get richer and the poor still get poorer.

This book, however, provides you with tools you can put to use immediately to increase your worth in the workplace. As an individual, there is not much you can do about the forces of globalization and the world economies. There *is* something you can do about *your* world and *your* economy.

The fact is, some people are making more and moving up in the workplace while others are not.

Sure, those born into the right families at the right time and in the right place seem to move up with lightning speed. In fact, sometimes it seems like they were born at the top. However, even those born at the top have to prove themselves. And if you weren't born at the top and don't start out with the right connections, that doesn't mean you can't move up.

As God's child, created in his image, you have certain innate gifts. But no one is perfect, and you have made and will make mistakes. Don't throw up your hands and despair; there is redemption and a way to start over, and you can start today.

This book contains secrets for your future career success. These are secrets your boss wants you to know. If you master every secret in this book, you will certainly experience positive changes in your life. And though you may not retire a multi-million-aire, God will provide you all that you need while you experience immense satisfaction and fulfillment from a job well done.

APPENDIX 1
Study Guide for the Seven Secrets

You can use this study guide on your own as you read and study the seven secrets. Use the following questions to guide your reading. Reinforcing the ideas found in this book, this study guide will help you discover ways to apply the seven secrets in your life.

If you are reading this book as part of a one-on-one or small group study, the study guide will help you prepare for small group meetings and could be used as a springboard for your group discussion.

Many of the questions in the study guide will ask you to think about changes you need to make in your life. If you are studying this with a group, it is my hope that you will find accountability within that group. Be sure to list very specific changes and goals so that your group can hold you accountable throughout the study.

If you study the secrets and make the decision to consistently apply them in your life and work, you will soon be on the road to success!

Introduction

1. When you hear the words "work ethic," what comes to your mind?

2. Do you tend to think of work as a form of suffering or as an adventure and a source of fulfillment? How have you developed this mindset?

3. List several ways in which God, in each of the three persons of the Trinity, works.

4. How does your perception of your own work change when you consider the fact that God also works?

5. What do you hope to learn from this text? How do you want to change as an employee or employer, working as one created in the image of God?

Secret 1: Change the Way You Think about Your Work!

1. Describe the "work ethic" in your own words.

2. Why is someone who does not have the work ethic immoral?

3. What does it mean that you are "wired" for work?

4. In what ways have you been able to enjoy the "fruit of your labor"?

5. Describe a situation in which you have ignored the work ethic. What negative consequence resulted from this situation?

6. What would you like to do with your time when you retire from your job?

7. Do your retirement plans line up with the work ethic?

8. In what ways has this chapter changed your ideas about your work and career?

9. What changes do you need to make in your attitude and practice to make the work ethic a part of your life? Be sure to write down specific, attainable goals.

Secret 2: Never Be on Time

1. When you arrive late to work, what does your boss think about your attitude? What does early arrival show your boss?

2. Are you a time-oriented person or an event-oriented person? What evidence do you have for your answer?

3. Is your boss or organization time-oriented or event-oriented? How do you know?

4. In the past two weeks, how many days did you arrive at work:

   _____ Late

   _____ On time

   _____ A few minutes early

   _____ Ten or more minutes early

5. List the reasons for each day that you were not early.

6. Do you think you should be paid for early arrival? Why or why not?

7. Describe your current morning routine and then describe in detail your ideal morning routine that will eliminate hectic mornings and ensure early arrival.

8. What changes do you need to make in your evening routine to ensure that you always arrive early to work and ready to take on the day? What specific steps could you take to accomplish this?

Secret 3: Always Be Positive

1. Have you ever voiced a complaint to someone at work about the job, your boss or another employee? Describe the situation.

2. Now that you know about secret 3, how would you handle this situation differently?

3. Why is complaining very dangerous?

4. List and describe three positive people you know and something they have said or done that has inspired you.
   A.

B.

C.

5.   Explain how you will respond the next time:
A. You are tempted to complain.

B. Someone criticizes you.

C. You are in a group and the conversation
turns negative.

D. You have negative or destructive thoughts.

6. List three pieces of criticism you have received recently (in a performance review or otherwise) that you could use to improve your performance on the job.

A.

B.

C.

7. In what ways do you promote your organization?

8. Decide that once per month, you will say thank you to your boss for your job and say something positive about the organization and/or your boss' leadership.

    List what you will say the first three months.
    Month 1:

    Month 2:

    Month 3:

9. Look up 1 Thessalonians 5:18 and Philippians 4:4. Write them out below, memorize them and recite them every morning and evening for 30 days.

10. What are some changes you need to make in order to demonstrate a positive attitude at work? List four specific things you will change.

A.

B.

C.

D.

Secret 4: Don't Be an Average Joe

1. What percentage of workers do you know who
    are Average Joes and what percentage have
    you observed always go the extra mile?

2. List three tasks that you recently completed at
    work or at home. Then describe what you could
    have done in each case to go the extra mile.
    A.

    B.

    C.

3. Check your employee handbook and list three areas where you could give 110% of the expectations or requirements.

   A.

   B.

   C.

4. In your life, what are your barriers to giving 110%? How will you eliminate these barriers?

5. Can you think of any personal or work-related projects you have begun, but failed to finish?

6. Why did these projects fail? What could you do to follow through with these projects?

7. Summarize in your own words what Brakel says about laziness.

8. Describe a "sluggard" in your own words.

9. How does thinking about God as your boss change your attitude toward work?

10. What specific steps will you take in order to give 110% at work?

Secret 5: Don't Bounce Around

1. How many jobs have you had in your working career so far? _____

    Divide that number by the number of years you have been working and write down the average number of years you spend at each job: _____

    Score: 10+ years = Excellent
    　　　　5+ years = Very good
    　　　　3-4 years = Good
    　　　　1-2 years = Fair

2. List the reason you left each of your past jobs.

3. Looking back, list those jobs where you could have or should have stayed longer and what you could have done to make that happen.

4. Would a future employer see you as someone who is "eager to jump ship"? Or have you been dedicated to your jobs and left them only for valid reasons?

5. If you had some short stays, how will you explain these in such a way as to assure a prospective employer that things will be different and that you intend to stick around?

6. Circle the qualities of a mature Christian that would describe you, especially as evident in your job:

Faithfulness	Loyalty
Dependability	Contentment
Perseverance	Patience
Maturity	

7. Considering your past work experience, try to describe the kind of job that would be your perfect "fit."

8. If your current job is not your perfect fit, in what ways might you just be "paying your dues"? What will be the benefits from sticking with it? How could you work toward your perfect fit at the job you have now? If your current job is your perfect fit, in what ways did you have to "pay your dues" to get there?

Secret 6: Become a Change Agent

1. Is your default mood change-resistant or do you have the attitude of a change agent? In other words, would you have asked why the ends of the ham were cut off?

2. List three good habits you have and want to keep and three bad habits you ought to change. Good habits:

    A.

    B.

    C.

    Bad habits:

    A.

    B.

    C.

3. Who are the chief change agents at your workplace? What do you admire about them? What could you do to be more like them?

4. Has the management made changes in your workplace recently that have been a nuisance to you? How did you react to those changes?

5. Put a check next to your level of completed formal education.

_____ High school diploma/GED

_____ Associate's degree

_____ Bachelor's degree

_____ Graduate degree

6. How much education would you like to have?

7. Map out a plan to help you reach that goal.
   Where will you study? How long will it take
   you? What will be your major or particular area
   of study?

8. What new experiences could you and your
   family have together to broaden your aware-
   ness of other cultures? Plan three activities
   that will expose you to new ways of thinking.
   A.

   B.

   C.

9. What Bible passages are especially comforting to you as things change around you? Write them out here, and memorize them.

10. Describe, as best you can, the vision your boss has for your organization, and list ways you can help make that happen from your current position.

Secret 7: Find a Mentor

1. In your own words, describe what a mentor is and what a mentor does.

2. Do you currently have a mentor?

3. In your own words, what is the value of having a mentor? Do you think having a mentor is important for your success? Why or why not?

4. List four people who have been influential (in a positive or negative sense) in your life. Then explain whether or not you see them as mentors.

A.

B.

C.

D.

5. What have these people done (or not done) that has influenced you?

A.

B.

C.

D.

6. List two living people you know whom you deeply admire and whom you'd like to imitate more. For each, describe specifically what they do that you'd like to imitate and why.
   A.

   B.

7. Write down when and how you will contact one or both of these people to make an appointment to discuss the possibility of meeting with them from time to time to ask their advice on various matters.

8. Read the biography of someone who accomplished something of significance during his/her life (e.g., Helen Keller, Martin Luther King Jr., John Calvin, John Wesley, John Whitfield). What could you learn from this person's life, and how can you apply that to your own life?

APPENDIX 2
Five Hints for Preparing
an Irresistible Resume!

Before you can become a success in the workplace, you need to gain *entrance* to the workplace. Usually, the first step to employment is submitting a resume. Your resume and cover letter provide a potential employer with a first impression of you, and most likely, these will determine whether you will be granted an interview.

I say "usually" because there are certainly situations in which you won't need a resume. The formality of a resume may not be required if the employer knows you extremely well and the organization is quite small. In most cases, though, be prepared to submit a resume.

Many places of business have an application for you to complete, which then functions as the resume. When applying to any organization, be sure you check if they require an application, a resume or both. Because employers design job applications to give them the same information about candidates as resumes, you can still apply these hints for preparing an application.

It is true that there are ample resources on the Internet about preparing a resume and cover letter. However, the hints here are less tangible and more difficult to find; they are truly secrets.

After each hint, there are a few questions to help you apply the secret to your resume. These questions will be most helpful for you if you have a copy of your resume in front of you. If you have never prepared a resume, take time to do this first, and then check your resume against these hints.

Use the application questions as you prepare your resume. Like the questions in the study guide, they will help you think about the ideas presented and will give you practical ways to apply these hints.

If you are studying this book in a group, these questions will help you refine your resumes together. Working through this section as part of a group will be helpful because you will be able to give and

He lied on his resume.
And he's not alone.

receive valuable feedback from the other people in your group.

I hope that you will find these five resume hints useful as you search for a job and throughout the interview process. Then, once you have accepted a position, be sure to apply the seven secrets found in this book, and you will be on the road to success in the workplace!

Resume Hint 1: Be Honest
Some studies indicate that up to 80% of people lie on resumes or applications. I once had an employee who claimed to have a master's degree, and I failed to check it out right away. When we had inexplicable problems with the employee (problems that made me doubtful he could have earned a master's degree from a reputable school), we checked and, sure enough, the school had no record of this person graduating. He lied on his resume. And he's not alone.

Recently the CEO of a large corporation did the same with respect to his education. When it was discovered that he lied about completing a doctorate, he was immediately fired. These days, you don't have to look far to find people who resigned, were fired or were denied jobs because of lies and "inconsistencies" on their resumes.

Lies about education are some of the most common lies on resumes. Other lies are more subtle: exaggerating the amount of responsibility in a previous position or the extent of involvement in a successful project. Many people believe that they will not be able to get a job unless they lie on their resume. I even found one website that *suggested* lying on your resume!

Because of the Privacy Act, it is sometimes difficult for a prospective employer to get information about you from previous workplaces. However, don't take comfort in that fact—an employer will find *someone* who knows you. Experienced personnel managers can also usually tell if something on the resume looks fishy, even if they can't quite figure out what's wrong.

If you lie on your resume, it will eventually catch up with you. If your lie is found out before you're hired, you can be sure you won't get the job. And nothing derails a career faster than having your resume lie found out while you are employed. If you want to be successful in the workplace, start with honesty on your resume.

Application Questions:

1. Examine your resume: Have you been completely honest? Are there any places where you have been dishonest in any way, including outright lies or exaggeration?

   Take time right now to fix your resume to make it completely truthful.

2. Consider this: Do you think it is necessary to lie to get a good job? Why or why not?

Resume Hint 2: Don't Hide Anything

Related to outright lying on a resume or application is attempting to hide things. Outright lying is the sin of *commission*; hiding information is the sin of *omission*. Frequently it is not, strictly speaking, being dishonest to omit some facts (no resume can contain *all* the information about you!), but there are *certain* things personnel managers don't like to see you hide.

For example, most employers immediately discard resumes that do not contain dates. Why? That's usually a clear sign that the applicant is trying to hide something. If you don't include the dates of employment at various places, your prospective employer knows that there are probably gaps in employment, brief stays or some other questionable reason for omitting the dates.

> *Being truthful shows full disclosure, which breeds trust.*

Older applicants may attempt to hide their age. Now, it is against the law in most places for an employer to demand to know your age, since this could encourage age discrimination. Even so, many people try to hide their age by omitting dates, such as the dates of graduation from educational institutions. Others try to hide their age by including recent college graduation dates and omitting a high school graduation date.

Keep in mind that although employers can't demand to know your age, they do have the right to know your level of education, the names of all the institutions you attended, your graduation dates and your previous work experience, including dates.

Although none of these "tricks" are outright lies, I would recommend that if something on your resume suggests your age, include it anyway, and let the chips fall where they may. Being truthful in this way shows full disclosure, which breeds trust.

Some candidates hide previous work experience because they have bounced around so frequently.

If you bounce around a lot, you have learned or certainly will learn that with each move, landing the next job becomes more difficult.

Rather than waiting until your boss finds out, it's better to list all of your work experience. Provide an honest and credible reason for your bouncing around and assure the prospective employer that you have learned your lesson and have every intention of sticking around for a while.

Sometimes an applicant will seek to be honest by listing only "relevant" work experience. This will hurt your chances just as much. Excluding some previous employment looks suspicious. Full disclosure is the key when it comes to applying for a job.

The only exception to the rule of full disclosure may be reporting time spent in prison or jail. Increasingly, employers are removing this question from their applications, realizing that if people have paid their debt to society, it is unfair to continue punishing them.

But many applications still include this question. The dilemma is that if you say you are an ex-offender, you almost certainly will not get the job. However, if you lie and your employer discovers your lie, you will almost certainly be fired.

If you have spent time behind bars, and a job application asks for your criminal history, I recommend that you write, "Please see me on this item" next to the question and hope they will give you a chance to speak in your defense.

The fact is, even if employers initially find a candidate who is ideal for the position, they will not hire a candidate who has been less than forthright with information on the resume. Such people can never be trusted on the job because, well, they hide things.

Application Questions:

1. Examine your resume: Are there places in your resume where you have omitted important information?

   Take time right now to fix your resume so you are not hiding anything important.

2. Consider this: If you have something on your resume that is potentially damaging (age, spotty work history, educational background, conviction of a crime), what legitimate explanations will you give to a potential employer who questions this?

*A flawless resume
shows what kind of
employee you will be.*

Resume Hint 3: Be Flawless

When preparing a cover letter and resume that will grab an employer's attention, it is of utmost importance to make sure you don't have any typos.

You would probably be surprised to know how many applications and resumes have spelling and grammatical errors. In a day when you have tools like "spell check" (though don't depend on that alone!), errors are unacceptable!

Why are perfect spelling and grammatical accuracy so important? Certainly there are many jobs in which writing skills are not necessary, but the details of your resume say a lot about you.

First, a flawless resume shows that you care! It shows that you gave it your best effort. Someone who doesn't really care about the job will rush through the application, but a carefully done, neat application tells the employer that you are serious about this job.

Second, a flawless resume shows what kind of employee you will be. If you present a carefully prepared resume, an employer can assume that you

*Be sure to have a
qualified person
"proof" your resume
and cover letter.*

will probably be an employee who is mindful of
details and willing to go the extra mile—something
employers love to see in their workers. Average Joe
doesn't bother to check the accuracy of his spelling
and grammar, but remember if you want to be successful, you will do *more* than Average Joe.

Third, a flawless resume speaks volumes about
your educational level. Your resume might say
that you have a high school or college education,
but spelling and grammatical errors will give an
employer a hint as to the quality of your education,
what kind of a student you might have been and
what you really learned. Not many things can
diminish the value of your educational history
faster than spelling and grammatical errors.

To ensure accuracy and to get feedback on what
you've prepared, be sure to have a qualified person
"proof" your resume and cover letter. Even the best
writers in the world have someone edit and proof
their work. Even if you proof it yourself (which you
certainly ought to do), there are things you may
miss, and it helps to have one or two other people
take a look at it for you.

Having someone proof your work, however, is a far cry from having someone actually write it for you. I once had an employee whose resume was flawless, but later it became evident that he couldn't have written that resume in a million years. Obviously, he had someone else write his resume so he'd have a better shot at getting the job.

This goes back to basic honesty and trying to hide things. Employers expect that you will have someone check your resume for you—that's why it should be flawless. But employers also expect you to do your own work. After all, the person who writes the resume is the person they want to hire.

Application Questions:

1. Examine your resume: Do you have any spelling or grammatical errors in your resume?

    Take time right now to proof your resume and have someone else proof it as well.

2. Consider this: How much of your resume have you prepared by yourself? Does it really matter who prepares the resume as long as the resume is truthful? Explain your answer.

Resume Hint 4: Research the Company

A sure-fire way to help get you an interview is to indicate in your cover letter and resume or application that you have studied the organization. Explain what you know and admire about the organization's mission. A potential employer will see that you resonate with the mission of the organization and will see your dedication.

You never want to submit a "one-size-fits-all" resume to an organization with a specific purpose. Generic resumes always end up in the "round file." Likewise, if an interviewer asks, "So, do you know what we do here?" and your answer is, "No, not really," you can pretty much guarantee it will be a brief interview. And a brief interview is usually not a good sign.

With the Internet, researching a potential employer couldn't be easier. Find out what the company does, explore the mission of the company and figure out what its goals might be. You should also research some of the top personnel in the organization, if possible. Doing your homework really impresses personnel managers. Your chances of getting an interview are infinitely greater if you carefully research and apply to a few organizations rather than emailing a generic resume to hundreds of HR departments.

Doing your research will also help you to find the workplace where you can be most successful. Getting up for work each day will be easier if you choose a job that you can do in good faith and an organization that you wholeheartedly support. If you know that the organization and its mission fit your goals and preferences *before* you begin working there, chances are good that it will be easier for you to follow the seven secrets, and you will find more fulfillment in your work.

Application Questions:

1. Examine your resume: Is there evidence that you have researched the organization and understand its mission?

   Take time right now to research the organization where you would like to apply, and update your resume and cover letter to reflect this research.

2. Consider this: How much research should you do before you submit a resume? Before you go in for an interview?

Resume Hint 5: Be Modest

A couple of generations ago, in many circles, children did not receive as much praise as they do now. Many parents believed that praise would make children proud, and humility was a prized virtue.

Then many psychologists began to worry about children's self-esteem. They advised parents to praise and compliment their children.

Now each generation seems to be praising its kids more, so much that Johnny begins to think he *is* the greatest and the best and is entitled to the highest praise and lavish rewards. Johnny enters the workforce and can't understand why his employer doesn't see him as "the cat's meow."

This entitlement attitude is often evident in resumes and cover letters. In cover letters I receive, a common sentiment is something like, "You will see by reading my resume that I am perfect for this position."

At this point I want to moan out loud.

Just how does this candidate know he or she would be a fit for this position, let alone a "perfect" one? That's what the whole interview process is trying to discern!

Regardless of how much praise you have or have not received in the past, remember that no one owes you anything. You may have some outstanding talents, but you also have a lot of areas in your life in which you are still developing and can still improve.

Yes, you want your resume and cover letter to emphasize your strengths. However, you never want to present your strengths in an arrogant or presumptuous manner. Instead, take what you've learned through your research, and demonstrate how you *might* be a good fit for the position.

You may even want to ask someone else to read your cover letter and resume to determine if they are overly braggadocian. In this way, you will achieve a balance between humility and over confidence.

Application Questions:

1. Examine your resume: Is there evidence of an attitude of entitlement in your resume? Have you included the phrase, "I am perfect for this job" anywhere in your cover letter?

    Take time right now to fix your resume and cover letter so they emphasize your strengths without swaggering.

2. Consider this: Do you think an employer would rather hire an employee that is too self-confident or too humble?

NOTES

[1] John Calvin, 2 Thessalonians 3:10, *Commentaries*, vol. 21, trans. Rev. William Pringle (Grand Rapids, MI: Baker Book House, 1979), 355.

[2] John Calvin, Genesis 1:30, *Commentaries*, vol. 1, trans. Rev. William Pringle (Grand Rapids, MI: Baker Book House, 1979), 100.

[3] John Calvin, Luke 17, *Commentaries*, vol. 16, trans. Rev. William Pringle (Grand Rapids, MI: Baker Book House, 1979), 195.

[4] Rick Pitino and Bill Reynolds, *Success is a Choice: Ten Steps to Overachieving in Business and Life* (New York: Broadway Books, 1997), 95.

[5] Pitino and Reynolds, *Success is a Choice*, 95.

[6] Wilhelmus à Brakel, *The Christian's Reasonable Service*, vol. 3, trans. Bartel Elshout (Pittsburgh: Soli Deo Gloria Publications, 1994), 190.

[7] Ursinus, Zacharias, *The Commentary of Dr. Zacharias Ursinus on the Heidelberg Catechism*, trans. G.W. Williard (Grand Rapids, MI: Eerdmans Publ. Co., 1954), 579.

[8] Calvin, 2 Thessalonians 3:10, 355.

[9] Brakel, *The Christian's Reasonable Service*, 222.

[10] Calvin, Luke 17, 195.

[11] "Pay your dues," *Cambridge International Dictionary of Idioms Online* (Cambridge: Cambridge University Press, 2010), http://dictionary.cambridge.org.

[12] John Calvin, Hebrews 13:8, *Commentaries*, vol. 22, trans. Rev. William Pringle (Grand Rapids, MI: Baker Book House, 1979), 345.